Woman, Thou Art Loosed! Workbook

T.D. Jakes

Treasure House

An Imprint of

Destiny Image® Publishers, Inc.
P.O. Box 310
Shippensburg, PA 17257-0310

"For where your treasure is,
there will your heart be also." Matthew 6:21

ISBN 1-56043-810-X

For Worldwide Distribution
Printed in the U.S.A.

Eighth Printing:	1996	Tenth Printing:	1996
Ninth Printing:	1996	Eleventh Printing:	1996

Treasure House books are available through these fine distributors outside the United States:

Christian Growth, Inc.
Jalan Kilang-Timor, Singapore 0315

Omega Distributors
Ponsonby, Auckland, New Zealand

Rhema Ministries Trading
Randburg, Rep. of South Africa

Salvation Book Centre
Petaling, Jaya, Malaysia

Successful Christian Living
Capetown, Rep. of South Africa

Vine Christian Centre
Mid Glamorgan, Wales, United Kingdom

WA Buchanan Company
Geebung, Queensland, Australia

Word Alive
Niverville, Manitoba, Canada

This book and all other Destiny Image and Treasure House books
are available at Christian bookstores everywhere.

Call for a bookstore nearest you.
1-800-722-6774
Or reach us on the Internet: **http://www.reapernet.com**

Contents

	How to Use This Study Guide	
Chapter One	Infirmed Woman	1
Chapter Two	Broken Arrows	3
Chapter Three	That Was Then	5
Chapter Four	The Victim Survives	7
Chapter Five	Walk Into the Newness	9
Chapter Six	Origins of Femininity	11
Chapter Seven	A Womb-Man	13
Chapter Eight	Anoint Me...I'm Single!	15
Chapter Nine	A Table for Two	17
Chapter Ten	Daughter of Abraham	21
Chapter Eleven	A Woman Without Excuse	23
Chapter Twelve	The True Beauty of a Woman	25
Chapter Thirteen	Every Woman Needs a Sabbath	27
Chapter Fourteen	Winter Woman	29
Chapter Fifteen	Breaking the Chain	33
	Answer Key	35

How to Use This Study Guide

This study guide has been uniquely prepared for the adult learner for personal or small group learning. As such, questions have been developed to allow you or your group time for discussion and application for spiritual growth. In light of this, it is receommended that you follow these guidelines:

1. Become aware of the book, *Woman, Thou Art Loosed*. Start with the Contents page and then familiarize yourself with the titles and subjects of each chapter.

2. Have your Bible, the book *Woman, Thou Art Loosed*, and the Workbook together with pen and pencil. Since satan would love to keep you from your growth in God, eliminate as many distractions as possible.

3. Read each chapter, looking up any Scriptures not written out in the book. Further, you are encouraged to use a concordance to check other Scriptures that relate to the ones being studied. Doing this can increase your depth of knowledge and understanding.

4. Answer the questions as provided in the Workbook to the best of your ability. Your personal answers can be shared with others at your discretion. However, sharing with and listening to others can increase your understanding as you struggle together with the concepts in the book and in God's Word.

I hope and pray that you will greatly benefit from the learning process, and that you will use the knowledge you gain for the Kingdom of God.

Chapter One

Infirmed Woman

1. A. What are the three main characters in the account of the infirmed woman in Luke 13:11-12?

    1. _____

    2. _____

    3. _____

    B. How do these characters relate to each other?

    _____

    _____

    _____

2. What is the prescription for any problem, even those rooted in the past? Explain using Scripture.

    _____

    _____

    _____

    _____

3. When Jesus "loosed" the woman, He spoke to the femininity of women. Discuss the importance of this action in light of today's society.

    _____

    _____

    _____

    _____

4. True or False. An emotional infirmity can be just as difficult to deal with as a physical infirmity. _____

5. A. When a person is hurting, how does she tend to use other people?

    _____

    _____

    _____

    B. What are the problems of doing this?

    _____

    _____

    _____

6.   True or False. An infirmed woman always lacks effort and fortitude. _____

7.   What was the root of the disappointment and depression in the life of this woman in Luke 13:11-12?

_____

_____

_____

8.   One of the great healing balms of the Holy Spirit is _____.

9.   Is there anyone in your life whom you need to forgive—including yourself? Take a moment and express your forgiveness for yourself and for that other person.

_____

_____

_____

10. How can a person, damaged by her life's events, be completely transformed into a whole woman?

_____

_____

_____

11. Discuss the grace and truth found in Jesus' statement, "Woman, thou art loosed."

_____

_____

_____

12. Discuss male/female relations in the light of uniqueness and unity.

_____

_____

_____

13. A. By nature a woman is a _____.

     B. What are the spiritual aspects of that truth?

_____

_____

_____

14. Explain this principle: Forgetting isn't a memory lapse; it is a memory release.

_____

_____

_____

_____

Further Challenge: Follow through on the book's suggestion to write down 30 things you would like to do with your life. Then check them off, one by one, as you accomplish them!

Chapter Two

Broken Arrows

1. Why did the psalmist David compare children to arrows (Ps. 127:3-5)?

_____

_____

_____

2. How would you describe a broken arrow?

_____

_____

_____

3. A. Compassion is _____.

   B. How does compassion relate to healing? Explain using Scripture.

   _____

   _____

   _____

   _____

4. Is pain prejudiced? Explain.

   _____

   _____

   _____

   _____

5. People have their own stories. Share (as you can) about any broken arrows in your life whom you've been able to touch.

   _____

   _____

   _____

6. A. Describe how Jesus ministered to the children brought to Him.

   _____

   _____

   _____

B. How does this challenge you in your life?

_____

_____

_____

7. A. Salvation is _____.

B. In what ways can you yourself be like a child in God's presence?

_____

_____

_____

8. Would you consider the pulling of misery from a memory as an event or as a process? Explain your reasoning.

_____

_____

_____

9. Think of a time when you experienced the security of God's arms. Describe how you felt. What did it do for you?

_____

_____

_____

10. A. What does it mean to be uncovered?

_____

_____

_____

B. How does God cover His people?

_____

_____

_____

11. For the hurting, God has _____.

12. Describe a time when God brought you or a family member through a crisis.

_____

_____

_____

Further Challenge: List some specific ways that you and your church can become more compassionate care givers to the "broken arrows" around you. Meet with your pastor and discuss the possibility of implementing some of these ideas.

Chapter Three

That Was Then

1. Describe some of your own spiritual "beginnings."

   _____

   _____

   _____

   _____

2. In striving for holiness, what were people actually trying to perfect?

   _____

   _____

   _____

   _____

3. How do you achieve holiness?

   _____

   _____

   _____

   _____

4. Describe the function of the Church in relation to caring for "people with a past."

   _____

   _____

   _____

   _____

5. A. Using the examples in the book or of people whom you know, describe some "people with a past."

   _____

   _____

   _____

   B. How can you respond to a "person with a past"?

   _____

   _____

   _____

6. We must maintain a strong line of _____ between a person's _____ and

_____.

7. What was it that Jesus understood about meeting people?

_____

_____

_____

8. The chains that bind are often _____.

9. Some chains can be from willfully _____.

10. What three things does Jesus come to do for the hurting?

A. _____ ____

B. _____ ____

C. _____ ____

11. What can women find as a result of Jesus' power operating in their lives?

_____

_____

_____

_____

Further Challenge: Name some things that keep the Church from accepting people with brokenness in their lives. What can be done to break down these barriers? Consider yourself as well, and begin to knock down the barriers you find in yourself.

Chapter Four

The Victim Survives

1. How does David's life show that children are most vulnerable to their father's weaknesses? Can you think of other biblical examples?

_____

_____

_____

_____

2. What is the difference between love and lust?

_____

_____

_____

3. What kind of healing does Jesus want to give?

_____

_____

_____

4. A. What is a tendency women have that makes them vulnerable to abuse?

_____

_____

   B. How can women safeguard themselves against falling into traps?

_____

_____

5. True or False. It is not your fault if you are being abused by being made a victim, but it is your fault if you don't allow God's Word to arrest sin and weakness in your life. _____

6. What are some ways God provides for healing and filling a woman's need for godly self-esteem and acceptance?

_____

_____

_____

_____

7. God's people are to _____ and _____ one another.

8. What does the statement "Love embraces the totality of the other person" mean to you?

_____

_____

_____

_____

9. A. What is the secret to being transformed from a victim to a victor?

_____

_____

_____

B. How can the Church be part of this process? Explain using Scripture.

_____

_____

_____

_____

C. Consider this process in light of your personal experience. How has the Lord transformed you?

_____

_____

_____

Further Challenge: List the characteristics of a person whom you could really open up to and who would help you go through the healing process. Are you yourself such a person? If you would like to be, what are some areas you need to mature in? If you are a victim, do you know such a person you could go to? Be encouraged to open yourself up to the healing process.

Chapter Five

Walk Into the Newness

1. Have you ever had anything happen to you that changed you forever? Describe the change.

    _____

    _____

    _____

    _____

    _____

2. What abuse did Amnon do to Tamar that was worse than rape?

    _____

    _____

    _____

3. The call of the Spirit to those feeling unwanted is "_____ _____ _____."

4. Describe how Jesus ministered to the infirmed woman of Luke 13:11-12.

    _____

    _____

    _____

    _____

5. Describe how standing up and living in the "now" of life is part of the recovery process.

    _____

    _____

    _____

    _____

6. It is Jesus' _____ and _____ that touches and heals the hurting places in a woman's life.

7. What else does God restore to your soul when He declares your freedom?

    _____

    _____

    _____

    _____

8.   What things should the Church, the Body of Christ, be providing for the hurting?

_____

_____

_____

_____

9.   A. List the three tenses of faith. What does each of these mean to you?

       1. _____

_____

_____

       2. _____

_____

_____

       3. _____

_____

_____

    B. Which of these is the most important, and why?

_____

_____

_____

Further Challenge: Instead of focusing on the tragedies of your life, focus on the victories. Make a list of the things you can praise God for, amidst the troubles in your life. Then actively praise God for them.

Chapter Six

Origins of Femininity

1. Women were made like _____; they were made to be _____.

2. In this respect, how is a woman a help meet to a man?

   _____

   _____

   _____

3. A. What is the vulnerability inherent in a receptacle?

   _____

   _____

   _____

   B. What is God's solution to this vulnerability?

   _____

   _____

   _____

4. True or False. Marriage will help an individual who is incomplete in her personhood. _____

5. A. How did satan "plug into" Eve?

   _____

   _____

   _____

   B. This has resulted in _____ between femininity and the enemy.

6. What must women do because of this conflict with the enemy?

   _____

   _____

   _____

7. How can you tell if something is "plugging into" you or not? Give specific examples.

   _____

   _____

   _____

   _____

8. Explain how suffering and sorrow are part of a spiritual birth.

    _____

    _____

    _____

    _____

9. For every struggle in your life, God accomplished something in your _____ and your _____.

10. God wants you to _____ the pain and _____ the baby.

11. In the analogy of the birth process, why is it necessary to push?

    _____

    _____

    _____

    _____

12. What is the balance that future desire provides?

    _____

    _____

    _____

    _____

13. Women of promise are "impregnated with destiny." How does this statement encourage women of today?

    _____

    _____

    _____

    _____

Further Challenge: Take a moment and examine your own life. Do you guard the point of access to your family? What are you allowing entrance into your life and family? Take steps to change what needs changing.

Chapter Seven

A Womb-Man

1. How is the desire to go forward intricately related to the power to create?

   _____

   _____

   _____

   _____

   _____

2. God wants to give us the strength to _____.

3. A. Vision is _____.

   B. Discuss the meaning of vision in light of Proverbs 29:18a.

   _____

   _____

   _____

4. A. What does God use to liberate us?

   _____

   _____

   _____

   B. Share some goals that you yourself have.

   _____

   _____

   _____

5. A. What must we put in our spirits to feed, nurture and allow faith to grow?

   _____

   _____

   _____

   B. Where do we get this truth? Give some examples.

   _____

   _____

   _____

6. How is faith like money?

_____

_____

_____

_____

7. Describe the way the lives of Abel, Enoch, and Noah present the relationship you can have with God.

_____

_____

_____

_____

8. Does a woman need a man to have vision and faith? Why or why not?

_____

_____

_____

_____

9. Discuss how faith, fear, and God's promises interrelate with each other.

_____

_____

_____

_____

10. A. When a broken person _____ to God, God gets the _____ for the wonderful things He accomplishes.

    B. By what means does God restore you and make you accomplish great things?

_____

_____

_____

_____

Further Challenge: Look at the relationship Mary and Elizabeth had. What do women today need to do to find similar sister friendships? What can you do to encourage such bonds between yourself and other women? Begin today to cultivate such a friendship.

Chapter Eight

Anoint Me...I'm Single!

1. Name some unique advantages to being single.

   _____

   _____

   _____

   _____

2. What should a single person's focus be?

   _____

   _____

   _____

   _____

3. List some personal, creative ways you, as a single, can minister to the Lord.

   _____

   _____

   _____

   _____

4. When you become faithful in your _____, then you will be better prepared to be faithful with a _____.

5. How does God view singles?

   _____

   _____

   _____

   _____

6. Is it wrong for singles to desire companionship? Why or why not?

   _____

   _____

   _____

   _____

   _____

7. The person who is single should be _____, not _____, in singleness.

8. Discuss some ways in which your relationship with God translates to a relationship with a husband.

_____

_____

_____

_____

9. What is the best example of the sacredness of marriage? Explain.

_____

_____

_____

_____

Further Challenge: If you are single, write a personal and intimate prayer of dedication to the Lord as a husband. Read it aloud to Him, and then sanctify yourself to Him.

Chapter Nine

A Table for Two

1. What was Adam's attraction to Eve?

   _____

   _____

   _____

2. Explain this statement: "When it comes to marriage, no one ever stayed together simply because they were attractive."

   _____

   _____

   _____

   _____

3. A. Everyone needs to pray and discern if their prospective partner is someone they can _____ to the rest of their life.

   B. *Debaq*, the Hebrew word for *cleave*, means:

   _____

   _____

   _____

   C. What is the secret to cleaving to a spouse? Discuss fully.

   _____

   _____

   _____

4. How does "The just shall live by faith" (Rom. 1:17b) relate to marriage?

   _____

   _____

   _____

5. A. How is suppressing your own sense of self unhealthy in a relationship?

   _____

   _____

   _____

B. What is the best way to deal with this type of relationship? Use Scripture in your answer.

_____

_____

_____

6. Describe the differences between the communication techniques of men and women.

_____

_____

_____

_____

7. A. List the four points of men's tendency to avoid open confrontation as revealed in Adam's confession.

1. _____

2. _____

3. _____

4. _____

B. What does a marriage need, in order for two people to deal with confrontation instead of hiding?

_____

_____

_____

8. A. What was it about Delilah that attracted Samson?

_____

_____

_____

B. What can married women learn from Delilah's example?

_____

_____

_____

9. Describe how marriage is a ministry.

_____

_____

_____

10. As a married woman, how would you rank your priorities?

_____

_____

_____

_____

11. In your own words, describe what it means to be married.

_____

_____

_____

_____

Further Challenge: If you are married, sit down with your spouse and really explore each other's way of communicating. Which ways work best for you? Then begin to practice communicating to bless your spouse.

Chapter Ten

Daughter of Abraham

1. Many see Jesus as a way to Heaven and the solution to _____ problems, but they fail to see that He is the solution to _____ _____ _____ problems.

2. Name some areas (other than spiritual) in which Jesus is our solution.

   _____

   _____

   _____

   _____

3. A. How much are we to want Jesus?

   _____

   _____

   _____

   B. What does that show about a person?

   _____

   _____

   _____

4. No matter what the problem is, _____ is the answer.

5. From the moment you are called to Jesus, you become _____ .

6. What can ensnare us and hinder us from becoming whole?

   _____

   _____

   _____

   _____

7. Jesus' power showed how powerless His critics' _____ was.

8. What must our ambition be?

   _____

   _____

   _____

   _____

9. A. Our _____ should not negate our _____.

    B. What is your position today? Whose are you?

    _____

    _____

    _____

10. Does gender matter when a person approaches God? Why or why not?

    _____

    _____

    _____

    _____

11. A. Faith is more than a _____—faith is an _____.

    B. Choose two people from the "faith hall of fame" in Hebrews 11 and describe their faith. How was their faith an action?

    _____

    _____

    _____

    _____

    _____

    _____

12. Faith is what _____ God.

13. If you want the enemy to release you, _____.

14. What must you do to receive what has been left to you?

    _____

    _____

    _____

    _____

15. True or False. It is what you say about yourself, and what God has said about you, that really matters.
    _____

16. Faith is the only thing in this world where there is _____.

Further Challenge: Are your words crippling you or loosing you? Take the time today to think about each thing you say—no matter who you talk to. What are you saying as you converse with your co-workers? Your friends? Your children? Your spouse? Correct whatever comes from your mouth that does not reflect your position as a child of the heavenly Father. Begin to speak deliverance and power.

Chapter Eleven

A Woman Without Excuse

1. A. How do attitudes affect your life?

    _____

    _____

    _____

    B. An attitude results from _____.

    C. Explain what perspective is.

    _____

    _____

    _____

    _____

2. We need to learn how to _____ _____ our perspective and _____ our attitudes.

3. True or False. People are supposed to function in life under the burdens of pressure. _____

4. How can a problem be an excuse? Share a personal example.

    _____

    _____

    _____

    _____

    _____

    _____

5. Before you can get out of trouble, you need to _____.

6. One of the greatest deliverances people can ever experience in life is _____

    _____.

7. Healing attitudes set people free to receive _____.

8. A. How can you protect yourself from accusers and negativism?

    _____

    _____

    _____

B. What must you do to allow the Lord to fight for you?

_____

_____

_____

9. A. Love is _____. It is not limited by _____.

   B. How does this concern marriage relationships?

_____

_____

_____

_____

10. How can the Church help the wounded?

_____

_____

_____

_____

Further Challenge: List some ways you can help change your attitude. Then ask the Holy Spirit for His help in reminding you about your attitude when you find yourself getting angry or depressed. When He does, stop and change your attitude.

Chapter Twelve

The True Beauty of a Woman

1. We must learn to _____ God for who we are…we must start _____ ourselves.

2. God put some things into the feminine _____ that a man needs more than anything God put on the feminine _____.

3. What does a woman need to know to be attractive to a man?

   _____

   _____

   _____

   _____

   _____

4. God has adorned the woman _____.

5. According to First Peter 3:1, to whom should a woman be in subjection?

   _____

   _____

   _____

   _____

6. A. What does the word *conversation* in First Peter 3:1 refer to?

   _____

   _____

   _____

   B. Why is this important in a marriage relationship?

   _____

   _____

   _____

7. What did Delilah give Samson that kept him coming back?

   _____

   _____

   _____

   _____

8. What valuable ornament did God give to women?

    _____

    _____

    _____

    _____

9. True or False. Sexual ability is more powerful than a meek and quiet spirit. _____

10. When are women daughters of Sarah?

    _____

    _____

    _____

    _____

11. True beauty is always _____.

Further Challenge: Do you know anything about painting and artwork? Find out how an artist goes about producing a masterpiece—how much time and care does he or she put into that one piece? Then consider how much more God has produced a work of art in you.

Chapter Thirteen

Every Woman Needs a Sabbath

1. The Sabbath is a day of _____. It is a day of _____.

2. It is during a time of rest that you _____.

3. Why do you need to rest your spirit?

   _____

   _____

   _____

   _____

4. What is another purpose for the Sabbath?

   _____

   _____

   _____

   _____

5. When is the best time to have God minister to your needs?

   _____

   _____

   _____

6. Describe some times of rest and God's refreshing that you have experienced in your own life.

   _____

   _____

   _____

   _____

7. Our Sabbath rest is _____.

8. A. True or False. The enemy prefers seeing you at rest. _____

   B. Justify your answer of 8. A.

   _____

   _____

   _____

9. Discuss how the perspective of the woman at the well changed from anxiety to peace.

_____

_____

_____

_____

10. When you get the _____, it gives you the _____ to let go of the _____.

11. The Sabbath rest is the _____ to find _____ _____ in _____.

Further Challenge: Having a specific time to rest and restore your spirit in the Lord is important for your spiritual health. Choose a time in your day when you won't be distracted and worship the Lord. Be willing to sacrifice to find this time and to make it a habit. The reward is well worth the effort.

Chapter Fourteen

Winter Woman

1. Describe the beauty you see in each season, as it relates to the life span of a woman:

    A. Spring

    _____

    _____

    B. Summer

    _____

    _____

    C. Autumn

    _____

    _____

    D. Winter

    _____

    _____

2. It is important that we teach women to prepare for _____.

3. Why should we spend more time encouraging older women?

    _____

    _____

    _____

    _____

    _____

4. Just because demands have _____ doesn't mean life is _____.

5. God tends to save the _____ for _____.

6. A. How did God restore purpose to Naomi's life?

    _____

    _____

    _____

B. What do you think would have happened if Naomi had persisted in being depressed and bitter?

_____

_____

_____

7. What other relationships are there besides family ones?

_____

_____

_____

_____

8. Describe the bonds between:

A.   Naomi and Ruth

_____

_____

B.   Elisabeth and Mary

_____

_____

9. There are two things every winter woman, every Naomi, can rely upon:

A.   God is a _____. What does this mean?

_____

_____

B.   God will be known as the _____. What does this mean?

_____

_____

10. Angels are the _____ of Heaven.

11. What is the purpose of angels? Explain using Scripture.

_____

_____

_____

_____

12. In a few sentences, describe the process Sarah went through from hearing God's promise to receiving the promise.

_____

_____

_____

_____

13. What did Sarah learn that all of us must learn too?

_____

_____

_____

_____

14. An example to women in every season of life, how is Sarah an example to you in your season?

_____

_____

_____

_____

Further Challenge: Look back to the friendship between Naomi and Ruth. If you are a winter woman, what are some things you can do to help younger women? What do you know from your life's experience that you can pass to others? Ask God to reveal to you His purpose for you as a winter woman.

Chapter Fifteen

Breaking the Chain

1. A. Why has the enemy concentrated on destroying women?

    _____

    _____

    _____

    B. What does this response say to your heart?

    _____

    _____

    _____

2. What has God done to meet your need?

    _____

    _____

    _____

3. Is there anything too great for the grace of God to forgive?

    _____

    _____

    _____

4. What happens when we accept Jesus as our Savior?

    _____

    _____

    _____

5. If the past is paid for, why then do we have scars?

    _____

    _____

    _____

6. God recognizes the _____ of what you can _____. He has a _____.
    He sees your _____.

7. What does God want to set free?

    _____

    _____

    _____

    _____

8. What can you do to respond to His call and be freed?

    _____

    _____

    _____

    _____

**Truly, you can do all things through Christ
who strengthens you. Woman, be thou loosed!**

Answer Key

Chapter One

1. A. 1. the person
      2. the problem
      3. the prescription

   B. For every person there will be a problem; and for every problem, God has a prescription.

2. A present word from God. God's Word, Jesus, is timeless; according to Hebrews 13:8, He is the same yesterday, today, and forever.

3. Reader's discussion.

4. True

5. A. As a narcotic to numb the pain.

   B. It does not allow God to heal a person; it can become addictive.

6. False

7. spirit of infirmity

8. ...forgiveness

9. Personal response.

10. By renewing her mind through the Word of God.

11. Reader's discussion.

12. Reader's discussion.

13. A. ...receiver

    B. Women must be careful what they receive; they must not allow the enemy to "plug into" their lives. They must receive only what agrees with the Word of God.

14. Forgetting is more than not remembering; it is letting go of the memory.

Chapter Two

1. For their abilities and potential for the future; for going where their parents point them.

2. Personal response.

3. A. ...the mother of miracles.

   B. Compassion allows healing power to flow; many times in Jesus' ministry His compassion preceded the healing (Mt. 9:36; 14:14; 18:27; Mk. 1:41; 6:34).

4. No. It affects the inside of a person, not the outside.

5. Personal response.

6. A. He stopped teaching, held them, touched them, and blessed them.

    B. Personal response.

7. A. …God giving us a chance to start over again.

    B. Personal response.

8. Personal response.

9. Personal response.

10. A. To be uncovered is to be unprotected.

    B. With the blood of Jesus Christ.

11. …intensive care

12. Personal response.

Chapter Three

1. Personal response.

2. the flesh

3. By receiving it by faith, and by allowing the blood of Jesus to sanctify the innermost being.

4. The Church is like a hospital that cares for people while they are in the process of becoming whole again.

5. A. Matthew was a tax collector who most likely gained his wealth by charging exorbitant taxes. Mary Magdalene was a prostitute. (Reader may have other examples.)

    B. Personal response.

6. demarcation; past; present

7. He understood the need to meet people where they were and to minister to their need.

8. …from events that we have no control over.

9. …living lives that bring bondage and pain.

10. A. forgive
    B. heal
    C. restore

11. the potential of their future

Chapter Four

1. David's weakness was a passion for women; his son Amnon also exhibited this passion. Personal response.

2. Love is a giving force; lust is a selfish compulsion focused on gratifying self.

3. Complete healing—in spirit, emotions (mind), and body.

4. A. their maternal instinct; also, a need for love

    B. by exercising discernment

5. True

6. Through a relationship with God as Father; also through platonic relationships with men.

7. nurture; protect

8. Personal response.

9. A. The ability to open your past to someone responsible enough to share your weaknesses and pains.

   B. Believers can listen to and help one another in their weaknesses, according to Galatians 6:2.

   C. Personal response.

Chapter Five

1. Personal response.

2. He did not want her.

3. "I want you."

4. He called her forward, waited for her to reach Him, then proclaimed her freedom.

5. Personal response.

6. power; anointing

7. joy

8. physical (platonic) touch; the Word of God; spiritual food; atmosphere of sharing and acceptance

9. A.   1. historical faith
        2. futuristic faith
        3. present faith
           Personal response.

   B. Present faith. It is current.

Chapter Six

1. receptacles; receivers

2. She is the receptacle he plugs into so he can meet and accomplish his task.

3. A. It is open to be plugged into.

   B. the commitment of the marriage covenant

4. False

5. A. He took advantage of her desire to see, taste and be wise; he caught her attention; he deceived her.

   B. enmity *or* conflict

6. They must do spiritual warfare.

7. By being vulnerable to moods, attitudes and dispositions; by doing things and not knowing why (for example, "I just feel like doing this").

8. Suffering and sorrow are the way through which a spiritual baby is born.

9. character; spirit

10. drop; hold

11. A baby will not come unless there is pushing; it is necessary to push in order to produce.

12. It gives the incentive to be productive again after the pain.

13. It gives a sense of worth and purpose.

Chapter Seven

1. It is when the desire to go forward is greater than the memories of pain that a person has the power to create again.

2. …overcome past pain and move forward into new life.

3. A. …the desire to go ahead.

   B. Reader's discussion.

4. A. a goal

   B. Personal response.

5. A. truth

   B. The Word of God. Deuteronomy 28:13; Psalm 8:3-4; 139:14; Philippians 4:13; etc.

6. It is the means, the tender, by which you receive the things you hope for.

7. Abel worshiped God by faith; Enoch walked with God by faith; Noah worked with God by faith. Worshiping comes before walking, and walking before working.

8. No. She herself can have faith; each person needs his or her own walk with God.

9. Reader's discussion.

10. A. submits; glory

    B. His anointing

Chapter Eight

1. A single woman can serve God with more freedom; she can pray, praise and worship God whenever and however she wants; she can build herself up in the Lord without other distractions.

2. The Lord and her relationship with Him.

3. Personal response.

4. singleness; husband

5. As belonging to Him.

6. No. It is a God-ordained need.

7. abiding; wrestling

8. Reader's discussion.

9. The relationship between Jesus and the Church. Jesus is the greatest advocate and intercessor for believers.

Chapter Nine

1. Her likeness to him.

2. A commitment requires an attraction that is deeper than outward appearance.

3. A. cleave

    B. "to impinge, cling or adhere to; figuratively, to catch by pursuit or follow close after"

    C. The secret to cleaving is leaving. Reader's discussion.

4. It is through faith that a marriage relationship can be changed.

5. A. It can lead to depression and will not guarantee an end to being hurt.

    B. To show by life style, according to First Peter 3:1-2, the purity and reverence in your life.

6. Men tend to be physical and women tend to be vocal.

7. A. 1. Adam heard God's voice.
        2. Adam was afraid.
        3. Adam was naked.
        4. Adam hid himself.

    B. The ability to be transparent; to expose vulnerabilities without fear or condemnation.

8. A. She gave him rest and cared for him.

    B. how to treat men like little boys, to give rest, to give safety, to praise, etc.

9. When you marry a person, you marry all of his past, his weaknesses, strengths, fears, etc. The things that need healing, you can minister to.

10. Personal response.

11. Personal response.

Chapter Ten

1. spiritual; all of life's

2. Finances, emotions, self-esteem, etc.

3. A. We are to want Him enough to overcome obstacles and to push in His direction.

    B. It shows how much they want help.

4. Jesus

5. ...invincible

6. our own words

7. religion

8. Jesus Christ

9. A. condition; position

    B. Personal response.

10. No. There is no discrimination in faith.

11. A. fact; action

    B. Personal response.

12. moves

13. ...remind him whose daughter you are.

14. You must ask for it; you must speak correctly.

15. True

16. …true equal opportunity.

Chapter Eleven

1. A. A good attitude can bring success; a poor attitude can bring destruction.

    B. …perspective

    C. Perspective is the way people look at life, which is often determined by their history.

2. look past; change

3. False

4. A problem can become a reason not to do other things, a reason for not changing. Personal response.

5. …straighten out your attitude.

6. …to have their attitude delivered.

7. …wholeness

8. A. By praising God, and not stopping.

    B. Quit defending yourself and attacking others.

9. A. eternal; time

    B. When you love your partner, your love covers everything—including his history and how it makes him react to certain things.

10. By sharing burdens, trusting one another, pointing to God, providing a haven of praise.

Chapter Twelve

1. thank; appreciating

2. spirit; body

3. To know who she is on the inside; to know her own self-worth.

4. …inwardly

5. her own husband

6. A. life style

    B. Unbelieving husbands watch their wives for their attitudes, dispositions, and words.

7. rest

8. a meek and quiet spirit

9. False

10. When they are not afraid, remain calm, keep control, rebuke fear, trust in God, judge God faithful, smile through tears, etc.

11. …on the inside.

Chapter Thirteen

1. rest; restoration

2. …replenish or receive back those things that were expended or put out.

3. It is through that rest that your life can begin to be restored.

4. for communion with God

5. when in real worship

6. Personal response.

7. …Christ Jesus

8. A. False

   B. He would rather break up your rest to keep you from being restored.

9. Reader's discussion.

10. best; power; rest

11. ability; eternal satisfaction; Jesus

Chapter Fourteen

1. Personal repsonse.

2. …winter

3. When they lose the people they built their lives around, they feel displaced and need new roles.

4. changed; over

5. best; last

6. A. He gave her a relationship with Ruth.

   B. Personal response.

7. friendships; "God-bonds"

8. Personal response.

9. A. …restorer; He restores purpose to the past and He makes up for the toll the past took on a person.

   B. …nourisher; He will care for and supply the needs of those who used to care for and supply the needs of others.

10. butlers

11. They are to minister to God's people, according to Hebrews 1:14. (Other explanations are possible.)

12. Personal response.

13. the faithfulness of God

14. Personal response.

Chapter Fifteen

1. A. They are God's vehicles of creativity.

   B. Personal response.

2. He sent a Redeemer, Jesus Christ.

3. No.

4. We are made pure; we become clean and holy.

5. Scars remind us that we are human.

6. possibility; become; plan; potential

7. The woman inside who can do great exploits in His name.

8. Have faith. Believe He will do what He said He would. Put your confidence in His power. Trust in Him. Believe He has washed you and made you clean. Believe He will satisfy every need.